The Day Sky Is Also Filled with Stars:

Love Poems for My Beloveds

The Day Sky Is Also Filled with Stars:

Love Poems for My Beloveds

by

Alinda Dickinson Wasner

Cover design by Shay Culligan
Cover art by Cindi Thornton
Author photo by Kathi Pontinen Hazlett

ISBN: 978-1-63980-384-2

Kelsay Books
502 South 1040 East, A-119
American Fork, Utah 84003
Kelsaybooks.com

For all my Beloveds

Dedicated to Hal and to all my children
and grandchildren

February 2023

All I ask of you is to remember me as loving you.

Contents

And There Is Eternity

(for my dear Indira)

And today she promises
she will go there
and buy the house back,

the one I sold when she was small
and live in it forever because
the bloom of light from the street lamp

outside the bedroom window
spun the curtains into gold
and in the deepest hour

the trains rumbled past
making the windows
sing a little tune

and the floorboards hummed
as if dreams
tunneled under

and we were safe there together
she in her little bed beside my big one
where we reached our hands out

and held on tight
until morning
painted the walls

so delicious a yellow
you wanted to lick them

and she swears she loved
the smell of moss
that made a tiny carpet

just outside the back door
(though I don’t remember this)
where the wind chimes

argued day and night
and the spruce trees
whispered the kind of secrets

that made a little river
inside her heart—
the same river

I kissed a boy in
when I was her age
and let him kiss me back.

Midsummer Love

(for all my MichiLuCa and Westminster friends)

What wealth!
That we can lie laughing
Under millions of stars
Calling each others' names out
In the dark
And naming constellations
After ourselves!

Oh, Friends, you cannot know
How your voices lifted in song
Are like the clear stream
How your laughter pitched on the wind
Surrounds me like extraordinary gods!

How your smile, quick as my True Love's hand
Reaching for mine
Brings me unspeakable joy!

First Loves

My mother's house
was crowded with so many things
there was never any place to sit
so the boy next door and I
squeezed into a rhombus of light
on the carpet each morning to play Jacks
and move his plastic Vikings
across an imaginary sea

And much later my first boyfriend
tried to kiss me
when he thought
she wasn't looking
but I saw her see,
her all-encompassing x-ray
vision like that of Superman's
ability to peer around corners and through walls;

So, when I notice my grandson
in the back seat today
curl his hand around his playmate's
and wrinkle his nose
close to hers,
I feel an angel in my heart,
its wings wisping
like a butterfly in the tall grass
on a blue-sky kind of day.

Wedding

Even before that
we walked on opposite sides of the street
arguing which was better
East side or West?
nevertheless, the friends threw rice
and it was everywhere—
our shoes our hair and later in the closet
and the suitcase
and how positively giddy we laughed as if
we had been drinking though I really don't
think we had
and you pulled the velvet gown with all those
velvet buttons up over my head
and read aloud from *The Song of Solomon*
and sometime in the middle of the night
you got up and ate what was left
of the tomatoes
and when you finally came back to me,
first brushed the rice out of the bed.

Sunlight on Oranges

In my grandmother's kitchen
Each crystal of sugar
A prism of desire on my tongue
Though she salted hers
Rivulets of juice
On her wrists, her fingers
Each plump segment
Pried apart by the knife, the point
Paring away flesh
The navel—she offered it to me saying it's what connected us
Her mother
Having died in childbirth and mine, well
What little we know
Maybe there were some regrets
The social workers
Never said much,
Lies mostly but now we have each other
And then her hands under mine at the piano
Lifting my fingers
Her voice in glassy arpeggios
Like the wood thrush
And soon the uncles on the porch
The smell of tobacco and starch
In the cool ironed sheets
And now the moon in the bed
And me clinging
At first to the edge
Until sleep lets me
Roll into her
Curl under that enormous arm—

And now today the tributaries,
The stain of raspberries
On my own hands
And on my own
Granddaughter's mouth
Brings it all back:
Love's first intoxication

Sundays

(an ekphrastic poem based on a painting by Edward Hopper;
to my grandparents who took us for those Sunday drives in the country)

At the halfway point they turned south
past the old barbershop, empty now
and the next-door bakery
where they used to always go
after church
and then East again
and at the intersection
rounded the curve where the bittersweet
burst into bloom and an old willow
wept over the culvert;

And they piled out of the car
and gathered the branches until their arms ached,
while on the horizon the clouds
dark and outlined in purple
looked more like mountains than clouds
and they were sure winter would be harsh that year
perilous
the cows in the field like a calendar painting
so much so that someone said the name of an artist
and everyone agreed,
while the old family house on the hill
stood silent, it's windows like broken teeth
the paint chipped and faded to grey
the path to the front door overgrown and
choked with chicory
and the grownups' faces seemed painted with longing;

But the idea of mountains
beckoned the children in the opposite direction
and they turned and flew—
little red-tailed hawks
swooping over the hill
until late afternoon shadows
slid over the mountains like smoke through the trees
and the last ray of sun
shone onto the grass like a searchlight through the clouds.

Both Our Hearts Crossways

Lying crosswise on the bed
Your head hanging over one edge
And mine the other,
The sky outside
An upside-down lake
And somewhere a lawn mower
Imitating a motor boat
And we float here a while
As if we have soared into another world
Which in a way we have, I suppose
You in the book spread open across your heart
And me thinking of those paintings
In the Louvre of Flying Lovers
A light breeze shifting the curtains
The harsh words we said an hour ago
Lifting and levitating like dust motes
In slant of sun.

Besotted

I suppose it was your sweet smile
When you first said hello
But when you saw my water skis
Remarked you'd never
Be able to paddle your canoe that fast

Or when you kept trying
To tell me how to do my job
(The one you wanted but I landed)
And I finally had to get snarky

And tell you you thought
You were God's gift to the woods
And so you asked me
To go out with you

But there was no place to go
Other than fishing
Though I hate
Fishing

So while you fished
I circled your canoe
In my best freestyle and backstroke
And when the big one actually got away

And your fish line
Snagged in the lily pads
I tried to work it loose
For you

But then you stood up
In the canoe
And it flipped you into the lily pads
On top of me

So we had to struggle back into the canoe,
While your pole sank to the bottom of the lake.
And when we finally righted the canoe it was flooded
So we had to sit on its floor

And swim it back to shore

But then came the summer storms
And the light shows followed by that horrible downed wire
Buzzing like a giant cicada
But after the lights flickered we still had power;

And to this day
We still get a lot of mileage
Out of that story
So that on wintry days

When we're at each other's
Throats over all things inconsequential
We can still take it out
And dust it off

While we tune in to You Tube
And watch *All This I Did Without You*
And remind ourselves
There is hidden treasure

At the bottom of the sea
And one day we might
Be able to get back there
And retrieve that pike

Still snagged
On the end
Of that damned fishing pole.

Baptism

At the baptism, during the blessing
My daughter, eyes brimming with joy,
Places her newborn son
Into the cradle of my arms
Saying, “He is mine *and* yours;”
And when the psalmist sings,
“There will be signs in the sun and moon and stars,”
My heart lifts and swells like the sea
As if a company of angels
Have already prepared a path
To lead us through the mighty waves.

Descant:

And I could come every evening
to look at the children
sleeping in their beds
my husband at the stove
preparing late night hot cakes
griddle steaming
and the dog curled
by the door—
Lord knows I have said terrible things
          to all of them
though I can't remember what, exactly—
all I know is,
the first time
I laid eyes on their faces
I fell so deeply, madly
in love I shall
never be able to extract myself
from myself
and for the most part
they seem to have
                    mostly loved me back.

Tonight There Are Stars on the Ceiling

(for all the grandchildren)

Blue ones and amber
Because the children are staying over
And the night light
Changes color every two or three minutes
And just when you think
The battery will wear down
If you don't turn it off,
You are suddenly too sleepy to do anything about it
And that's when you notice the children are already dreaming
And if you don't close your eyes they will be up before you know it
Begging for pancakes and scrambled eggs and the oldest will want bacon
And suddenly you realize
This is what the Poets meant when they wrote about happiness
And maybe even ecstasy
These sleepy faces around your bed
Saying wake up now the birds are singing the morning songs!
So you put on your bathrobe and fuzzy slippers
And make your way down the stairs
Holding hands with the littlest because this
Is what you have always imagined love would really be like
And suddenly you realize you were right.

Euphoria

O, Love, love
That idea
That comes and goes

A construct, creation myth
Lust and lemon
Whisked and troubled over

Sweet concoction,
A meringue
Of longing—

So when a recent bridegroom
Asks if I felt different

After I was married
I tried to think
A yes, but no,

Perhaps a reach, a grasp, a shrug
But I confess

When first we waltzed
Into that Garden
There may have been

A tree, the fruit,
Perhaps even a serpent
Although the cake

Was sheer perfection
As was the velvet gown,
The sky a frosting

Over all the earth—
But who can say for certain
If I was giddy

With anticipation
Or illusion
Or merely fearful of the ordinary

Always hovering,
Threatening to settle in?

Open Boat

The slow music of waves
Carrying us to the depths
To the clouds
Indistinguishable from sea
And the rocking, pitching,
Lapping laughter of friends
Echoing across the water—
And lanterns on the prow
Flickering like fireflies,
Like stolen kisses
Under a confetti of stars
Breaking over our hearts
Like 4th of July celebrations
A parade of planets
Bursting over the horizon
So we cannot tell
War from celebration;

And my husband tells the story of war
Of living in a potato cellar
When he was three
Certain a bomb would fall on his head
And I think of my dear youngest grandchild
Who cries into my shoulder
Because he is afraid
Of fireworks, thinking gunfire
And to this day
My heart
Shatters like glass

With the reverberation
Of boots on pavement
In military parades:
As the soldiers of death
Salute an evil general—
The one who ultimately
Comes for us all.

First Day

Trust him to the elements
The long walk to the school yard
He says he's ready
Has been looking forward to this
For so long
Back pack heavy for small shoulders
But he's eager, red shirt bright
In morning sun
The *Book of Pirates* on the floor
Where he left off
Wondering if he could pick his own teeth
With a sword, walk a plank
Hoist a mainsail
He knows he can do them all and more—
Because the world is ready if you are
And I suppose
My own mother watched me go:
The schoolyard waiting
And I see now
What she saw
The sky embracing
A sea so blue and swelling
In all its dangerous and glorious pride.

Wizard

Today he's in the culvert in his red jacket, oblivious to the last of the melt oozing over his boot tops, oblivious to the cold and mud, intent only on gathering ice fragments on the tip of a stick he found on the lawn, last summer's sword now transformed into a magic wand, a divining rod that he points at the water and the heavens, the late afternoon sky so blue and brilliant a fresh painting that only Michelangelo could have mastered and I smile at a possible title, *Boy in Spring* or *Last Rites of Winter*—either way, I go back to fixing dinner and when he comes in soaked and shivering, I towel him down and get him into dry pants and shirt and lift him to the table where he reaches for the soup and biscuits and after the first bite smiles at me and says, you know I am a lot like Moses, don't you?

For All the Saints

(for Carl, Dear Dad, who loved without question)

After Mom died
Dad walked across the road to The Family Dollar
And bought one of those candles in a tall jar with a cross and a
picture of a saint,
Placed it by his chair
And kept vigil every evening for a year
Sitting in the dark with memories he never shared
Nor did I ask
And after the year passed
Threw it into the trash
Along with the photos of their life together
Replacing them with
The few he had of his own family—people I'd never seen or even
heard of
The little room a sudden sanctuary
And when I asked, he
Spoke tenderly of his childhood, poor as he'd been,
Recounting his father's inability to hold a job
And his mother's struggle to hold the family together
By peddling pies at the train depot
And his own paper route that afforded him the luxury
Of piano lessons though
He never mastered the left-hand register
So took up the mandolin instead
And learned all the old songs
The accordion voice of the wind his only guide
But it was enough, he said,
To understand the few words about love and sorrow
And know not everyone would always get them right.

Ferris Wheel

The first time to the top
The pause Just before the

D
r
o
p

and I understand that love is a Carnival—
the blue ribbons
calliope,
cotton candy—
all there in the pit of the stomach
almost seasonal!

and how could I not crowd in line with the others—
the excitement of queuing up
for a tornado in a tea cup
beside a boy with ruddy cheeks
and secret kisses
as startling as a gunshot.

Over time I've confused him
with the fire in the tent.
the lion's roar,
cigar haze,
and ice cream
melting in the moonlight:

a long unending arc of happiness—

and the ticket still warm in my hand
on the long walk home.

Divertimento

Breeze out of the south today
licking the windchimes
and the waves
spilling over each other
like lion cubs
before the play gets too rough

and on just such a day your kisses
like margaritas
salt the edge of my mouth
hint of summer limes

while over your shoulder
the sun, a lipstick smudge, on the horizon:
a small flame about to die out

High School Tromp L'oeil

Standing on the steps of the high school those mornings I envied the other girls
their eyes lined and lips glossed with 79-cent Avon—and while Jane argued with Priscilla
about which was more seductive, intelligence or the new math teacher,
or when Pat bantered with Bill about batting averages and RBIs,
I wished I too could get the hang of small talk;
instead, tongue-tied, I resorted to noticing how the older boys, pants pegged
and hair slicked back like Elvis, followed the curve of light on a cheerleader's sweater.

Those afternoons Warren and Jeff chained their Harleys like wild animals to a tree,
and, collars turned up, danced unafraid in the gym;
while, out on the ball field, trombones growling and trumpets howling,
the marching band, deployed between grandstand and goal post
toed the twenty-yard line tonguing triumphantly the truculent high notes.

Even then we understood some small secrets about passion
and long before someone smuggled the D.H. Lawrence from the Latin teacher's purse
or lifted the *Ulysses* from Mr. DeWalt's personal library, we were already worried:
that hope had an ablative absolute, that regret was its own intimate,
read infinite, series of vectors and trajectories.

What we studied was not just Joanne's impeccable grade point
or John's infatuation with physics;
but those nights, Lucky Strikes smoldering under the streetlamps,
we worked hard to perfect the algorithms of our own lies and legends.

What we learned was that our teachers may have seen us
with more compassion than we allowed ourselves or one another;
what we still want to know is how to convey all of this,
now more than thirty-five years later.

Love

Sunlight, hum of bees
clouds on edge—
Lick of heat lightning up the spine
And the air all
Secretive
Birdsong through the trees
Like spilling water
The scent of fresh grass
Like adrenaline in the veins
And somewhere the wind
waiting
With its kiss.

Ode to the Night and the Morning Following an All-Day Day of Arguing

rejoice for the thick turn of wrist, for nut-brown skin,
black coils matted under the wristband
rejoice for the smoothness of cheek pressing into the pillow
for the Picassoesque close-up of the lover with three eyes
for the hand that knows just where to tempt
and for fingers flying over the keyboard of the body
rejoice for the willows slow-dancing slow, slow, slow-dancing
slower in the moonlight
rejoice for leg pressed against leg
and the high-pitched whine of blue notes
sliding out of an 18-wheeler down-shifting like a harmonium out
on the highway
For the familiar mouth and whispers having finally replaced
the god-endless pontification
rejoice for chickadees chikkerring in low bushes
for the dead mosquito no longer zizzing
for shadows half painted in moonlight
for the night grass gossiping to the neighbors
And rejoice for the moon sneaking in, under, around, and through
the branches
fingering the edge of the water
for the basso profundo of a slow-moving freighter
for sweat and juices pooling in all the right crevices
rejoice for the moon and the sun and the morning stars sneaking
into the bed with us
For nights that end too quickly but for a hot wind kicking
the sheets into a tangle
And rejoice for the cool side of the pillow
for the jay shrieking Me, me, me ME
loud enough to obscure the cry of arching bodies
from the neighbors

rejoice for the sound of the cimbalom and the click
of the CD still skipping
rejoice for the DNA of thick ankles
for eyes dark and quick as a junco's
rejoice for new sun in the cattails
for poppies pole-dancing in upside-down red skirts
For irises with their beards jutting
and green lingering in, under, and, around night's edges
and rejoice the whisper of breeze cozying up again to the willows,
begging for the slow dance to start over

Sonogram Song:
The Aria

I am singing you, Child, the moon a bride still veiled in the
heavens, calligraphy of clouds writing me toward you in 3:00am
blizzard—on such a night so cold and brilliant my own
firstborn delivered and again now no lane markers no taillights
ahead just my own heart,
loud rushing planet!

Ah! love's dangers—the winds in full swirl, zealots inciting, but
sin boldly! said Luther this journey a new psalm for the *Book of
Generations* Ours, Yours and Mine, World without end, Amen!
"Idolatry of the child!" cry the protesters—stay back, turn to bed—
wait for reasonable (Herods in their nightshirts!)

O, Mary, mother of god I confess it! *Amo, amas, amat!* who am I
to question 1:00am phone call, the heart's eagerness? What is
black ice in the face of Love's gale, what matter a little car
spinning like silly sperm, swerving into the night sky giddy in
grandeur!

So let us sing this child sleeping in translucent basket in crowded
nursery, little dawn feet kicked free of swaddling blankets,
overhead lights blinking good news: he is ours! *OURS!*
that one! out of danger! red-faced and squalling!

We know him already who nested under my daughter's breast as if
my own heart beating—wild bird! common and extraordinary
his mother in half dazed sleep love-drunk and dreaming,
Angels singing their sonogram song, Earth's sonorous hum so low
and steady

And all around us the world in full chorus of stars   libretto and descant *sforzando* for all new days dawning, foretelling the day when we hold hands around a table and you, barely two, tell God how happy you love me and at three, clench my hand beg me, plead,
Please not to be really, really old

just a little old please! your heart so too early wise to shattering but hope, that which
passes all understanding: and at four you still   unreserved and full unembarrassed   bestow tender heart smiles given for me   you still unsuspecting other loves in your future

And I am singing you, Child, Holy Innocent, Unadulterated, into my past and your future this very moment, this joy of daysong of moon high and bright in afternoon sky and you in my arms and the daystars, the heavens, so dazzling and full glittering like new snow, swirling around us,

sequins and seed pearls enough for a thousand brides' veils
glistening on the heart of the world   World so dazzling and so full of splendor! My soul uplifted, lifted up in wonder!
Our hearts in the updraft!

The First Time I Really Notice You

you are carrying in
a box of Halos
and artichokes
looking for somewhere
to put them
though god knows
there's no place
to set anything
in this kitchen
an old box
of kosher salt
having turned to granite
on the counter top
and the Pisa of empty
cottage cheese cartons
leaning on every available
surface as if
they've been here
since the Depression
which they very
well may have
alongside the mountains
of newspapers and professional journals
and you say
this has got to
stop
meaning this place
where your family lives
is such a mess
you're embarrassed
for me to
have to see it
and you have
said this before

and now I have
this sudden need
to defend your mother
to tell you
the old adage
about the woman
whose home
is so ready
for the unexpected
guest she’s too
tired to entertain
because mostly I want
to make you laugh
I want you to
find me attractive
I want suddenly
to take the box
from your hands,
peel the oranges
cook the artichokes
just for you
assuming you like
artichokes
assuming I’ve ever
prepared artichokes
but I could learn
though mostly I want
to take your face
in my hands
your hands
between mine
hold my palm
to your palm
and peer into

the blue world
of your eyes,
measure the curve
of your mouth
with mine, I
want to confess
all things indecent,
press your hair
to your head
just to
see it spring
back into place
watch the way
you stretch your arm
behind your head
as if reaching
for an arrow
from a quiver
a modern-day David
your gaze fixed
on some distant idea
lord knows why
I want to go
crazy with love
or
maybe I just
want you
to explain the physics
of probability
it could be a TED
talk—a half hour
to an hour
designated to sustain
my desire for

the mere sight
of you coming
through that door
with oranges
and artichokes
a pink residue
of light from
the ceiling fixture
on your wonderful
hands
your kind smile
as you see me
see you for
the first time
come through that door.

Neighbor Boy

Always the mysterious one
Said his parents drugged him
When he was a baby
And hid him in the trunk
So he wouldn't cry
When they crossed the border
Who, when he is thirty
Shows me a news clipping
Of his family on the last transport
The one Shanghai-ed in China
The only port that would accept them
And when he asks me to dance
Junior year
I can't remember
What I wanted to ask him
Except I suspect he asked me on a dare
And I hate the beautiful blue dress
He says reminds him
Of the ocean
And I hate my father
For spending so much for it
My father who refused
To ever talk about war
Who gets up and leaves the room
When old Army buddies
Start talking about
Who they gun down
In darkness and daylight
And only recently
Have I seen photos
Of the prisoners he helped release
From Mauthausen
And only now I recall how he walked to work

Every day at the coat factory
In our small town
With my friend’s dad
Still new to the US
Who may or may not have
Shared the story
Of his boy swaddled
And barely breathing
When it was safe enough
To open the trunk
And sunlight swirled around them
As if the ocean would swallow them whole.

Life on Kercheval and Harding

Though our parents thought it was a nice enough place and we were happy exploding water balloons on the back lawn then came Gasoline in 7-up bottles finding their way through the neighbors' window and their house with its eyes blackened and teeth missing though over time we sometimes forgot there was always an undercurrent of darkness on the brightest day. little stress and inlets of worry we could read in their faces despite the happiness we allowed ourselves making chalk flowers on the driveway pretending we didn't see the gangs of boys sauntering through the alley, cutting through our side yard to the street as if they owned it which they pretty much did but sometimes we went to their parties knowing they weren't allowed to carry their guns into the house so hiding them in the bushes by the front porch until we were gone, our mother standing nervously on the sidewalk the whole time keeping her eye on so many situations and sewing yellow curtains for the dark kitchen so there would be a slant of light in addition to the ceiling fixture with its hoard of dead flies and mosquitoes and we scoffed at her over our soup because we figured she so often worried unnecessarily and the guys with Saturday Night Specials usually shot themselves in the foot and though I loved James Freeman and he loved me back there was always the outline of something heavy in his jacket but I promised myself never to ask him about it.

Little Thieves

Were we eight or ten the year the Young Boys
Moved in down the street
Fencing stolen stuff in the dark
The catalpas
Bulging out over the sidewalks
Like bouncers at an all-night club
Seed pods littering the lawn
Like gang signals?

By winter, rumor had it
That the kid who'd
Robbed all the Free Press paper carriers
In the neighborhood
Was now on the FBI's 10 Most Wanted list;

And so I never told anyone
How outside the school one sub-zero morning
He let me warm my hands
Inside his mismatched mittens
While he tried to lick my face
As if I were a Tastee Freeze—me being
The only white girl on the block.

And I never mentioned how he howled—
(Some said like a pregnant cat)
When his tongue froze
To the little bridge over the canal
And bled onto the snow like graffiti
When he tried to tear it away
Before the hook and ladder men arrived,

Nor did I ever mention anything to him, either,
How his fingers not much bigger than mine, really
Had curled so softly around my hand
Just before the entry bell
Buzzed us all into the school
Or how sorry I'd been at the last minute

To have to pull my cold hands
Out of his warm ones
Or how, after he dropped it on the playground,
I put one of the mittens into my pocket
And kept it. And never gave it back.

The Heart Always Lingers

(from an ancient folk tune)

And when I woke
we were lying on a magic carpet
beside your bed
your mouth on mine
and how we got there was a mystery
and if it was your dream or mine
I had no way of telling when we'd entered
or would leave
or if we were simply always there
like in a painting
a streak of sun across a canvas
it's just that we were so much younger
when even then I thought I didn't stand a chance
and maybe never will
but I am wild with gladness for your sudden smile
and the light through trees
outside your window.

Inspired by Oystein Savag's *My Heart Is Always Moving*

Too Much Happiness

Dew on fresh cut grass
And new day
Honey-warm and slow-spreading

Bees buzz-buzzing in Granny's lilacs
Hum, humming
Old ancient song

And, somewhere
A radio
On neighbor's window ledge

Playing *Whenever I See Your Smiling Face—*

And this day like every other
We girls and boys
Filing in and out of Scripps Elementary

Morning sun all gold medallions
On windowpanes
Sea-smooth blue

And starlings stuttering in catalpa trees
As cars careen down Kercheval
Speeding off to work

Drivers dance-jiving
In they seats!

Jackhammer staccato
Bass and blues
Like train engines in the bones

And, Oh! We just so happy
Being children
Teasing each other merciless

Clouds telling little white lies
In damp-bright
Early morning air.

For Erich

After the sun goes down I
Lie in my son's bed and listen
To the noises of the house;
Things seem different from the left—
My husband's foot upon the stairs
My daughter's laugh

My room is to the right of things
But here in the evening in his place
I wonder what he heard of household noises
Smelled of smells
Even the neighbors seem closer here
Perhaps he knew them (better than I)
Better than I thought I did.

Here in my son's room it is hard to know
What memories to keep, which want for sorting out
Even the dust seems to know
It must replace him
Still, somewhere under the fresh paint
There is a boy's laugh
Blue and wet as the morning we moved in

Rising up as if it were meant
To catch in my own throat
And what I know of time, like rain,
Will settle down to dust
To keep, to wait.

Scheherazade

And, oh, that time
the husbands were away,
(who can remember where?)
and we rolled up the carpet
and pushed the furniture back against the wall
and someone brought out finger zills from her purse,
and another reached up under her blouse
and whisked off her bra
and we all laughed like the girls we once were
and for an entire night we belly-danced to Hachig Kazarian and
    Ramzy
and shimmied around the room
until we were so hot and sweaty
I threw open the French doors to the back yard;
and after we danced some more,
we lay on the grass under the silver maple in full moonlight
each leaf shimmering like a silver Judas coin
and the branches dividing the sky into constellations
as if from a chapter in *1001 Arabian Nights*
and for a while we took turns being Scheherazade,
telling each other the reasons why our own husbands
might think they would have cause
to have us sewn into the carpet
and thrown into the Bosporus come morning.

Light from Light

Whatever his language didn't really matter and we laughed
because the bed was too small for
the both of us and in the dim light of the lamp with the tilted shade
I could read his smile and whatever gods we worshipped laughed
with us that rainy afternoon in that seventh-floor walk-up where
the key turning in the lock sang a little tune, barely decipherable,
but nevertheless an ode to all rainy afternoons still to come.

Wonders to Behold in the Summer Sky

(for Alex and Lara)

That summer the blue spruce were mysteriously starting to die
And the wind spent most of its time
Chasing its own tail back and forth across the bluff—
Even so, the pollen clung to all the window screens
And the backs of our throats
And because you were only two
It fell to me to keep you safe for five weeks
While your mom had to
Go away that first time;

And to keep you happy and distracted from the pain of missing
her,
The pleasures of the first week,
The finger painting
The little tent we pitched on the porch
The endless balls and books and blocks
The wading pool,
A train we made of cardboard boxes
All worked their magic.

But in the second week you
Started to call me Mommy
So I'd wait to reply until you self-corrected.
And that week we made endless trips to the library
And to the play parks
And a farm
And took little hikes through the woods
Past a little cabin where you said maybe the three bears once lived
And later we gathered river rocks
And splashed them with water paint
Which kept you fascinated

And, blessedly,
Tired you out just enough
To sleep peacefully
At nap time and bed time.

But in the third week
Your eyes dimmed
And words wilted
Like late summer flowers
In a too-delicate ecosystem
With too much sun and rain
And even the crickets
And cicadas, once so insistent,
grew so suddenly silent;
And all I could think to do was hold you
And carry you everywhere
As we sat on the swing overlooking the lake
And tell you stories about
Stones that could sing and stars and comets that ran away
And joined the "*circusclouds*"
And you found shapes in the daytime sky
Sheep, goats, dragons, dogs
And after dinner we counted fireflies
Until our eyes grew tired
But when we couldn't sleep
Took our flashlights down to the river
And counted the fish
That were already sleeping
In the cradle of the moon upon the water.

And then the sun grew hotter, so hot we could barely breathe
And, you slept and slept
And so did I

As the last two weeks
Slid slowly by as if a bee stuck in honey
On a breathless day
We might never recover from.

But then, when we least expected
She came back.
And as you clung to her neck
In fear and delight
You told her everything—
Your words so precisely calibrated
To insist how when you were her age
You read all the books
In the library
And that you dreamed every night
She had stars in her hair
And when the moon rose high in the sky
You became a fish
That slept in the water
While the crickets
On the riverbank
Sang silly songs
That made you laugh even in your sleep.

And she laughed;
And you laughed
And we all hugged
And laughed til we finally cried
And light from the summer stars
Wrapped the house
In a silvery scarf
And the wind
In the trees

Blew and cajoled and finally pulled us apart as gently as it could
Until my sight of you gradually disappeared—

And to this day
You say you really don't remember any of these things
Except the wind
Whistling at the window
And perhaps the fish
Sleeping in the sunlight.

But then you've heard the story
So many times
Your heart believes
That because I'm the one who told you
All these things
Some of them might possibly be true.

Some Times

I take a little detour
down your street
past the houses
where we played
Priest and Martyr
the lawns more lush than ever
and maples
still dropping
their scarlet leaves
the moths
flitting through the grass
where you fell
that day
when your heart
just stopped
suddenly
and we all laughed
because we thought
you were
joking
like the time we'd practiced
kissing,
your lips
almost on mine
whispering little secrets
we were
still too young
to understand.

Housesitting for the Neighbors

(for Lara)

My daughter wants a house
like the Apters'
she wants to come home
at night and sink down
into the warm brown
velour of dark
she wants to stretch
out on the rug like a cat
to sip tea
out of champagne glasses
she wants the people
in the photos
to claim her
to come down from the wall frames
and say yes,
you are ours now
you were meant
to sustain this
the fingerprints
could be yours
there are rings on the tables
from the soupbowls
just like your house,
you are ours.
My daughter wants a house
like the Apters'
she wants smokecurls
in the chimney
she wants sisters
who will let her be the oldest

she wants windows
that turn out to a world
that is different
and a piano that plays by itself
a tune
that is new
and unbroken
my daughter wants a house
like the Apters'.

Chaconne

Today the neighbor to the left of us is playing Buxtehude's *Toccata* on his Steinway, the one he hired a crane to hoist through the third-floor window of his flat, the breeze blowing the notes through the linden trees so gently even the starlings are silent which is saying something.

Usually, children fill the street, chirping in competition, but they are in their beds now, as charmed by the exotic notes drifting through the air as those of Hamelin must have been.

I was in his flat once having been invited up on a bright summer morning allegedly for tea to hear him play only to be startled by an odalisque sleeping on a mat beneath the keyboard, its lid open like an impolite yawn.

Don't mind her, he said, she won't bother anything.

And so he played an allemande and a five note fugue and the sun through the window sparkled on the glass that became a river of daystars across the floor; and when he turned the page as lightly as if he were lifting the hem of my dress, I understood why I could sleep there, too.

But my husband was down below tilling the garden much like Adam must have after the fall; but for now I was simply Eve, still too naive to understand the implication of desiring more days like this to come.

And Where Was I Going with This?

(for my sister, Rusti)

Oh, yes, the pink hotel, ghost condo, I think Miami,
Where so many were being built
But so few occupied
And the thieves-in-training
Running through the intersection
Pretending to be hit and maimed
The drivers fooled into stopping
Long enough for the "injured"
To speed away with the car—
And those little
Hole-in-the-wall restaurants
Where cabbage and onion sandwiches
For fifty cents were the all rage
And the used bookstalls with mountains
Of paperbacks strewn on the ground—
God knows we thought ourselves wealthy
As we lugged all we could carry up three flights of stairs
Then raced back
To gather up more,
Ecstatic to be newfound friends.

Antiphon for the Long Way Back

The long way back always has its price
As does the way forward

The measure of sun
exacted in rain drops and clouds
the cost of stars immeasurable;

And when I behold you falling from the sky
I pay the price for encouraging you
To fly, O, my child, the wings you want

Are still too big for you
Your need too great
For what little I have to give

But the wind in the trees outside my window
Still plays its tunes for you
Still sings your name

Even in the gentlest breeze—
Even when you are far away from me
When the notes fall from the flute

And the last page of music,
I will gather them up
And put them back on the staff for you—

So you can rearrange them
To your own satisfaction
For your sweet voice

Still calls to me across the ages
In the way only you know how

And I am always here
Waiting to hear you
Once again say my name.

What I Longed For

And still do
Is always to now and then
Hear the descant of your boy's laugh
Above your newly acquired man's voice
And the rapture
Of your daily adventures
As you shared them each afternoon
When you burst through the back door
Dropping your school books
On the floor by the kitchen table
And poked your head into the fridge
For an after-school snack
While regaling me with your incredible insights!

Oh, Child, let me relive your enthusiasm
For all things Einstein and Egyptology
And all those schoolboy puns
About "Crook a diles" and "Invest a gators"
And Spiders
And, okay, farts
And about the new kid you think is incredibly cool

And I promise not to tell you until thirty years from now
How I parked two streets over from the school
On occasion
Just to see you lope by
For those few moments
With newfound friends and old,

As you tossed your head back
With joy
At an inside joke
Or intimate secret that
I can only guess at
As you pursued your newest dreams
And adventures—

Even now, I rejoice with you all the same!

Late May

(for Lara, who, like her father, is always late!)

Early morning slash of light across the field
and the small trees trying on their little leaves
that will take a few more days
to unfurl
And my daughter in her party dress
the shiny shoes
sparkling as she twirls
a little carnival playing in her head
This child who will grow to sass me back
to declare I don't understand her and never will—
and she could be right—
But the important thing
Is she is
Who She Is
Smart and beautiful
And will never be bound to calendars
Or clocks
The second hand marching on
Without her
The sunlight
Always in her wake.

Refraction

(for RM and PR)

Like the moon on late night water
My memory of you keeps breaking:
First light, then shadow
And always
The unbearable space
That holds the two
Together

Had Things Been Different

(dedicated to Irish author William Trevor)

Had things been different
I might have run off with him
As was my first inclination
But that would have meant
Leaving the children behind,
My book unfinished

And spring was in full bloom
The cottonwood spilling its seedlings
And all that "cotton" flying with the bad
Company of the willows, the fluff
Sticking to our eyes—

And maybe if the birch trees and alders
Hadn't been shedding
Or the oaks filling with staminate flowers
For the second time
And the grasses releasing so much pollen
We might not all have been
So completely miserable

I could have just disappeared
Mid-morning or evening
The dog in the yard, the children
In the shadows, porch lights
Just coming on
And the seventeen-year cicadas
Ratcheting up their relentless refrains;

Given the right circumstances
I suppose I might have been happier
The sunsets brighter
The days more exotic—

But bring me the book again
That I might reread it
Might find myself on a different page
Find him somewhere in an adjacent chapter
The corner turned over
My name still emblazoned
On the flyleaf of his heart

Because We Could Fly

No one thought to ask
How or why or when or even if
We were coming back
But as far as I was concerned
Never would have been too soon
Quoth the Raven
Or whomever
Didn't much matter
As long as you understood
Even if I returned
I could never be fully present
Having sung with birds and angels
And laughed with God
The old fart
Who slapped his knee
When you least expected
And stole the joke without
Giving credit
But over time you forgave him
The guffaw, the wink
The criticism, the commands, commandments
All of it still fresh in your mind as if you'd
Splashed in the pool
Of childhood together
He with his pudgy hands
And soft, sweet smile,
That time he pinned
A poppy in your hair
Just behind the ear
The wind in the tall grass
A kiss, the kind that mothers
Brush against their infants'
Heads, eyes closed,
The bliss of peonies
Nodding in the Garden.

The Creek That Sang Out Your Name

We are standing
down where the sand is wet
where the creek that happily sang out your name,
daylight or dark
and spring peepers
made us laugh—
But I've forgotten until now
how angry I was at grownups
who told the children whose parents died in a car crash
that mommy and daddy were stars in the sky
winking down;
But when you were three I capitulated—
When I am old, I said,
and you are sad that I've gone from here
look up! Second star on the right
that's me!
tell me a joke and we'll both laugh—
And although this is the year you've outgrown me
and I've tried not to grieve
just when I think I've lost you completely
you're here suddenly
no longer silent
telling me about the books you now love
and the movies
and you describe
a computer game you will write
in which I will be Indira Gandhi
and you will be Alexander the Great
and we will make world peace;
And for the half day we are together
my heart swells with happiness

while you describe how you don’t like
to be held to a schedule
and that lately you’ve been thinking
about the little cottage where we stayed
and how you still recall a cold, loud-sounding
river and spinning planets that followed a deer path
along the bluff
where we sat in a tree
that leaned out over the water!
And the wind carried our voices up to the clouds
and while we waited to see if they would return,
we held hands and counted the stars in the sky
knowing each one had a story of its own to tell the universe.

How Could You?

Leave so silently?
How could all those years go by
without me knowing?
without me telling you
I love
your imitations of Moliere
your tears over *Ethan Frome*
and the way you teased
about Denzel Washington
leaving his shoes under my bed?

How could you go
with all that James Baldwin and Thomas Hayden
still undiscussed
a second and third time?
and Toni Morrison,
especially her!

Did you not know
I loved the notes you wrote
in the margins
praising the words
I'd worked so hard on,
your script tidy
and meticulous
as your thoughts,
the questions you asked
as precise as an orator's?

And the way you glanced
at me from time to time
when you thought I wasn't looking?

Heat Lightning

(for DKE)

Every afternoon at same time between low-low branches, licking down our road enough to scare the *bejeezus* and we afraid to walk between them for fear of going up in smoke or strike dead whichever come first and Auntie say God give the little pickney the whitest hair and the fairest of them all a Cupid face and black kinky hair so the neighbors all wag their tongue and say My, my and did the evil fairy in the castle make one never cry and the other be all crybaby and who the Daddy some say the preacher but he disappear and the sun sink into the sea they sky all blush embarrass and we giggle at the bare ass part but Auntie put a stop to that she say stop or she send us all to Canada where some white Granny teach us lesson and we say no thank you, Miss Pearl, who be our mama but not really, some high-tone lady by name of Ruby be our real Mama like princess in a castle and some day she send for us and we say, No-no thank you anyway we see your picture, that hat, big feather, some fox bite-bite its tail 'roun your neck, but we happy here the cocoa trees all brown and buttery, the sky all blue with rain, same time each day and the heart some days still hope she come herself to get us if she really love us.

Kites

(for all families who have lost a child or children)

That fall how you flew toward the river
The wind lifting you up one side of the hill
And nudging you down the other
Filling all the children's jackets like little balloons
Pushing some of them onto the grass
And others into the hedge that surrounded the hospital
That was closing the children's wing—
And we prayed the prayers of the weak, the hopeless,
The adamant, the unbelieving
The sinner, the saint
Each beat of the heart a bead on a rosary
Against the blue of sky, gown, surgical mask, even the room
To which we had promised
To return you at the end of the day,
But now no longer could.
And when we held you in our arms
You were lighter than a bird, yea
Light as a cloud
And breath flew out of us
On wings of blame and recrimination—
Our thoughts dull as rusty knives
That we would somehow have to sharpen
Once we got back home.

Full Moon

Today he tells me when the moon is full
He follows the path to the top of the mountain
And when the time is just right
He steps into the yellow door and once inside

Looks out over all the world
And watches us dream
Saying he can see everything
In our dreams

And sometimes he gazes down
At his own reflection in the sea
A big yellow beach ball the size of a sailing ship
That, depending on the clouds

Sometimes smiles and sometimes laughs
And maybe even frowns
But it is a good way to understand
The meaning of the world

And do I know I sleep with one foot
Kicked outside the blanket
Just like he does, and his sister?
And that he figures it's a sign

Of that hot-but-cold-at-the same-time feeling
And that people who sleep in the shooting star position
Are open to others and generally very amiable, likable people
He, on the other hand, is what you could call a yearning dreamer

But sometimes a skydiver-stomach-sleeper
A real risk taker, if you will,
And do I know that he likes to live dangerously
Sometimes, but mostly in his dreams?

But usually he worries
About how to get back down from the moon
Without falling into the sea
Because he knows his mom wouldn’t know where to find him

Although once he fell out of the top bunk
And landed on the blue rug on the floor
And she almost stepped on him
When she came in to wake him up.

Wander

Down the hill from the stand of red pines
where the path opens to bog lilies
and tamaracks at water's edge
knee-deep in swamp mallow,

we swam in deep spring-fed lakes
under the blue bowl of sky
and swore undying love
to the red-wing blackbirds

that swooped from cattail to cattail
singing their bawdy songs
and cedar waxwings played dart tag
through the tall grass like stealth bombers

but mostly we dived like ospreys
into each other's eyes
singing at the top of our lungs
all the songs from the Old Country

the ones we promised to teach our children—
then floating in silence to determine
if humans had magnetic force enough
so that ultimately our heads would point due north,

And after that we lay in the sun
on the hillside until the moon rose in the heavens
and stars enough to name constellations
after ourselves

and all the magic in the universe,
shone down on us
as we understood, if only briefly,
how important the grandeur and fullness of love.

Just This

The long river thread
Always unwinding itself from hem of day

Reds and scarlets
Of earth's fall finery

And that one sweet memory of you
The two of us hand in hand at river's edge

Sun and moon both in the late afternoon sky together
And we watched a school of little fish

Sleeping in the cradle of the moon,
The sky

So gently
Lowering its purple and magenta scarves

Around our shoulders
As if a prayer shawl,

A benediction
For another glorious day

Together!

Connections

(formerly "Eyelid")

Today the youngest says what if the universe
is a giant eye with an eyelid that unzips
each morning to let the sun and the birds out
and tries to close at night
but can't because there are so many
stars and planets jam-packed
they spill out like tears
so even if you keep trying you would never be able to find
enough glue or safety pins to
help hold it together
and did we know the invention of the safety pin
is what caused the Industrial Revolution?

And I marvel how schoolboy brains
spin constantly like a centrifuge,
how a bazillion ideas for inventions keep him awake half the night;
so, when my husband jokes (I think he is joking!) that it's
impossible
to brush your teeth in outer space
without getting toothpaste up your nose,
I tell them it's a myth that you'll fry to death if you get sucked out
of an airplane
(because it's actually worse than that).

But of course they merely scoff when I later threaten
that if meanwhile they don't pick up all those damn socks lying all
over the floor
the evil dryer fairy will stick one sock of each pair up their noses
when they're sleeping.
and the resident smart Alec says that's totally ridiculous
because everyone knows it's really front loader washers that eat
sock families

and, besides, why do I care so much about mismatch when our
family is already mix and match
and we can't afford an expensive washer in the first place?

But just then the teen daughter, having had quite enough of family
quarreling by now
suggests maybe we'd all of us be better off if we'd just focus on
the fact that a Moon
masquerading as a giant Mylar balloon
is stuck in the tree at the end of the road and shouldn't we at least
call 911 or NASA
to check on the daily lunacy level of this stupid family
before we get all bent out of shape over the unimportant stuff?

When I Was a Boy

Wind in my pigtails
and me careening around the corner
on Billy Borgan's bright blue boy's bike
and he on my new pink Schwinn
until his mother puts a stop to that
saying I am a bad influence
even though he always chooses me first
for his sandlot team because he says
I am the best hitter
best retriever of flies and grounders
better than almost
all the other boys
everyone except him
and because I let him
handle the tools my dad
lets me keep
(even the Scout knife with all
those blades and openers)
and when we
climb the ladder to the cherry tree in
in our side yard,
and sit in the branches
we stuff our mouths
until the tart, sticky juice
covers our chins
and runs down our arms
and drips off our elbows
as if our veins
would explode
with all the laughter and love
in the universe,
the first breeze of afternoon
a tender, stolen kiss

the likes of which my
son will one day tell
me about as he
mentions his new friend,
one with a girl haircut
or a boy's
he can't tell which—
does it matter?
because he already
knows it's someone
he will most definitely love forever.

Tonight at the Jazz Festival

I search the crowd
For your face
Recalling the
Warm-cool breeze
That riffed through
Your hair
Like hands
Skimming a keyboard
While miles of notes
Spilled wildly from a trumpet
Like white water rapids
And then slid seamlessly from a saxophone like long silk ribbons.

Until just now I'd almost forgotten
How,
In the shadow
Between two trees,
We swayed to the flame
Of a candle set on a small table there just for us
And the wind's

Too-quick kiss
On my shoulder then, as now,
Made me somehow think
I might find you here
Again, years later
On a same but sadly different
Cool-warm evening.

Moon

And today he tells me
That sometimes when he can't sleep at night

He slips out his window
And climbs the hill behind the house

That on some nights reaches as high as the moon
And when he gets to the top

He goes inside and looks out
Over all the world

And watches everyone and everything dream—
The trees, the animals, insects, and flowers

And did I know there are also stars that take turns sleeping
Because they get tired from all that twinkling?

And I say I climbed up there once myself when I was five
But I couldn't get in because girls weren't allowed to in those days

And he says that was a long time ago
You're old now things have changed, so we'll go together next
time

I'll hold the door for you—

And ever since then, whenever the moon
Shines outside my window,

I think how wonderful it will be
to climb all the way up there with him

And watch over him when he goes back down.

The First Time You Really Notice Me

I am standing in your kitchen and who's to say there's not a moment of whiplash as I notice you notice, not that there's anything out of the ordinary though I'd like to think it's my blue dress or the fact that someone just told you so I could overhear he'd once been in love with me, or that I asked you for your recipe for the May wine infused with sweet woodruff, (whatever that is); after all, you've known me for years but never seemed the least bit interested but a room infused with late afternoon light can cast a spell so subtle that one might decide to listen to Beethoven or Chopin though the old piano is silent, the piano scarf a dusty prayer shawl embroidered with ancient letters and the breeze through the open window a wish, fingering the fringes with a lover's touch.

The First Time You Say My Name

I am on my way out your door
The one that sticks and
Requires a full body slam going in and a tug of war going out
Though I have done it
A hundred times now but
Once in it's usually just hello or a quick good bye
And sometimes a few pleasantries in between
Because after all I'm just here to be neighborly
Although one time I gave you a CD
And you showed me a project you were working on
And another time I borrowed (and returned) a book of theory
Without asking your permission
Not that I understood much
Except that you studied long and hard
To perfect your technique
(Though it seems somehow inborn)
Nevertheless, I have memorized your quiet manner
And once I dreamed you were kissing my eyelids
A sort of jazz riff in an upper register
But now that you've said this
Or at least the way in which you've said it
The moon and stars go suddenly transparent
And the evening breeze and newly fallen leaves
Write poems on the pavement
As I make my way home
And even without a backward glance
For the tiniest split second
I sense your door still open to this warm September night.

Sweater by My Feet

Under the sheet
At night when the bed is cold
Better than a cat I think
The dog snoring lightly
On the floor next to me
And the grandson in the little bed
Across the room
Asks for a story
About when I was his age
And because I've already told him
Most of them, he will sometimes
Correct a detail or two or a plot twist
Or supply a metaphor
And I have to laugh
Because I didn't have siblings
No one to know or
Remember
Any details of my days
And I am careful to be truthful
Even about the time
I was so mad at my mom I slammed the back door so hard
The glass fell out and shattered
Clanging like wind chimes as it hit the driveway
Or the time I defied her
By riding my bike to school
On black ice and skidded and fell
In front of the school bus just in time
For it to honk and pass right over me
Like a dark angel and slam into the telephone pole
And I was shaken but unhurt
So got up and ran
Entering a side door instead of the main entrance just as the
principal

Announced that he needed to know the name of the person
Who caused the accident,
And the blood in my veins
Turned to ice
And my mouth remained silent
But no one came forward
And though someone leaned my mangled bike against the curb
I pretended not to see it until one day it was no longer there
And even when my best friend said it sure looked a lot like mine I said nothing
As we stepped through heavy snow
And the winter storm erased all of our footprints
By the time we finally arrived home.

Angelus

(for my first grandfather, Alan Ricker, who held me to his heart on the freezing cold day I was adopted but died when I was five)

He says the world is new with her in it holds her hair to his face and breathes deeply and outside the window the hay newly mown the old people praying in the field as if in a famous portrait he is so thankful he celebrates the sun in the kitchen, on the walls, drinks his water with sugar pours sugar into the milk every drop so sweet the sky like spun sugar the baby in the cradle a little sugar doll he could lick until she disappears and the woman he loves so perfect for babies he could faint with thanksgiving and desire and the raspberries so heavy on the bush the fields abundant with early potatoes this time of year he knows She was made for the garden, created for the fields, the first time he saw her disappear into the corn, her braids the color of sun he was afraid he'd lost her that she would never know his desire so he ran to find her, panicked when he couldn't, got down on his knees, when he finally did, breathless and apologizing for no ring but she'd already bought one for herself and he fainted with joy didn't care if the world knew his weakness and in the end for lack of pride pounded on the door of the upstairs bedroom all morning cursing for her to let him out but she was in the barn for the milking, hurrying through the chores anxious he'd hurt the child so fierce was his love and only after she took him the cup of new milk, sloshing over while she ran, watched while he filled it with sugar, drank as if his thirst would never be quenched drank until he held the empty cup out to her and begged for more and More before he calmed down, smiled at her so sweetly she didn't know what to think the doctor said sugar would kill him the sore on his foot would not heal he could no longer stand it, no longer stand on it, the stench when he took off his boot like that of rendered hog, summer swamp, there was no answer to their prayers the child younger than three when it happened, when she came out from the barn, found him in the yard, lying on the moss-covered flagstone on his back like an angel smiling up at her so sweetly she thought he was dreaming, the grass shimmering with emeralds and rhinestones the flagstone a bed of stars from the upstairs window, glass all around him sparking like the little chips in her ring and somewhere the squall of a new baby she knew she had to get to but first she couldn't leave him all alone out here in the grass, the fields drenched in sun, the sky an ocean ripe for spilling, about to burst with so much blue.

The Way to Be Happy Is to Always Be in Love

And today he tells me the stars in the river of his heart
are all exploding because there's a brown-eyed girl at his school
that he has a crush one
someone he's asked his best friend
to tell her he really likes her
and the friend
has asked for a return favor regarding
a cute blue-eyed blond
and though he won't tell me her name just yet—
(until just recently he's always told me everything)

how well I remember the first time he pointed at the night sky
and exclaimed, *stars!* with sudden recognition
and the little notes I'd find with the squiggly hearts
and letters of my name on them all askew
tucked under my pillow
and how, upon falling into bed at night we'd declare
our love for each other all the way around the universe and back
naming each planet until
invariably I fell asleep first;

And oh! I tell him, did I ever tell him
about the first time I really noticed
the Jewish boy who lived down the street
5th grade I think it was,
who told me Torah stories
and once inked my name in Hebrew letters
around my wrist like a bracelet
and declared his undying affection
that made me almost pee with happiness
but later broke my heart?

But now that the moment has arrived,
that some sweet young thing
has stolen my darling boy's affections,
I see that my predictions were pretty much right on target—
that though I'd always known I'd always be his first love
(not counting his mother)
I at least lasted until he was twelve!

Crush

And today he tells me
He's about as happy as he's ever been
And I believe him because lately
He's been humming as he reads
As if the book is filled with secret music
And he's learning the tune
And in the same breath he mentions
A cute girl at school
And asks me what is a crush
And how do you know if you have one
And that all the stars in the river of his heart are exploding
And is the way to be happy to always be in love?
And immediately I think of the portrait
Of the handsome ancestor he most looks like
Smiling seductively from the mantel
And wonder how to explain
Something so wonderful as
Sunlight slanting
Through gauzy curtains
Caught in a summer breeze
The whisper of leaves
High in the trees
The creek
Tumbling happily over itself
And somewhere
A thrush singing its heart out
Deep in the forest
Its bold and glassy arpeggios
For any and all to hear.
And I remember the first time
He pointed at the night sky and exclaimed
Stars! (Was he yet two?)
And who until now

Has always claimed he loves me
To the moon and back
And I hope this girl will be so delighted
The first time he says this to her
With his shy glance
That she could almost
Pee with happiness
And I hope she is the kind of friend
Who before they break each other's hearts
Might at least now and then give him a chance or two
To let him win at Chess or Scrabble or Nintendo.

Gun Play

(for all children killed by guns)

Seven candles
And the birthday boy
All excitement
And lightheaded
As Mylar balloons
Drifting to the ceiling
His fingers such
Sticky swirl through
Blue and chocolate
Just as his friends
And cousins arrive
And thinking
He'll join the song
Sing his own name
Loud and clear this year
Let his mama
Hear the reverberation
In his own heart
Today and all tomorrows
And his Daddy's piece
Tied up in the closet
In a shoe box
Where no one needs to know
But he's already
Told the boy
Who just turned nine
And made a pact
To trade it for Nintendo

When the grownups
Drift out back
For beer and ice cream
And his own tongue so silky-sweet
At the back of his throat
In the
Last few seconds
Before the blast
Of music
Can silence
All suspicion.

Need to Know

In the Bible, all the critical stuff happens on a mountain
and when you ask me to go climbing with you I envision a basket
with monks and hermits pulling us up to the top
but you have been training and all the muscles in your arms and shoulders and abs
make you a perfect Goddess, Athleta, on the cover of that catalog with everything Spandex
and though there are accounts of voices in clouds and interpretations and extrapolations galore,
we're all too quick to assume the voice belongs to God though there's nothing in the text
that actually says that, and because you are my daughter, I worry endlessly about The Fall
and how that time you plunged from the table top in your infant seat onto the tile floor
before I could catch you
after that I became a mother lioness, would have carried you by the scruff of your neck
for the rest of your life, licking the hollows of your throat and sending you forth
in a suit of armor with a check list that said you are not allowed to play in a house that has a gun
and if you dare to set foot on a freeway
I will smack the bejeezus out of you
but then the day you disappear and fliers go up on every lamppost and the Amber Alert people rally round, I am beside myself with grief because you had told me you were running away but I instead made a wisecrack
about be sure to write to me when you learn how
and then twelve hours later find you asleep on the back seat of my car where for some reason no one thought to look, your little suitcase packed with Barbies and mittens and that look on your face that said wherever you were going you had somehow figured I would drive you,

and praise be we live long enough to laugh about it
so now when your own daughter so full of 9th grade sass and teen sex makes you say you want to say those words about someday her having a daughter just like her, I tell you I tried so hard never to say that to you
like my mother said to me
But if I'm honest, I confess that more than once I most surely thought it

Love, Love Love

It's simple, he said
    It's not that I don't love the old me
    Just that the new me is so much better.

As If Just Part of a Book
(For My College Crush)

Late morning—the phone—
my name like music
from your mouth,

castanets, my heart
flamenco dancing!

And yet remind me, Someone, please!
the human heart is the same size as a fist!

And, wouldn't you just know, today's clouds in all the Heavens
shiftless in the heat

scowling a grey and dubious
kind of sky Morse Code

dot dot dot, dash dash

Like Lightning striking twice
in my stupid brain

Against my better judgement

And now the remnants of irony:
hot summer flat

cool sheets
Loud fourth floor music!

Silly me, to trip and fall for
an impish grin, a gap-tooth smile

Such ludicrous lust
and laughable!

And do I put the phone down,
let thunder drown the ringing?

Your ass gone halfway round the world
now mouthing epithets so insatiable, old Love so ruinous!?

And after all this time!
(Oh! How could you?)

Three's a Charm: Three Little Etudes

I

Café Amour

And maybe we'll go from here to your room
To test the theory that coffee and a nap
Inevitably lead to love stories
Each of us in a starring role

II

Just Temptation

   even if we used *Google Translate* and you said to me in French
      what I long to say to you in English
         we can never   because desire can wreak
so here we are at a loss because if we do say
         we'll have to act as if we never did

III

Storm

White caps on the lake and wind blowing in from the Nor'east,
   clouds all tangled in little white lies getting bigger,
   sun sputtering out and the weather channel showing rain
   with knives in it slanting sideways,

   fog predicted, low visibility,
   warnings to keep off the water, stay out of it,
   rip tides on the increase:

      Love. What else is new?

To Alexander Who Is Turning Nine

Who wants to know
Who is my worst best friend
And was I ever accused
Of something I didn't do
And if so, what
And would I rather jump out of a tree
Or take a mud bath
And what was it like the first time I knew I was adopted
And if Donald Trump closes Anderson public school
Will his Jewish and Mexican and Arabic friends be deported
And why do people say he's black when he's really just tan
And did I ever talk back, why or why not
And why does he have to take music lessons until he's fifteen
And what was it like when I got to the hospital the night he was
  born
And can decimals be even and odd numbers
And what if verbs that are irregular are really just constipated,
  haha?
And why do I have to be so old that I could die
Before he gets married
And what was the best book
I ever read
And do I know what year Pokemon was invented and
That Albert Einstein didn't like wearing socks either?
And I tell him
Nine is such a good year for answers and questions—
Which does he think is more important?
And he laughs and says,
Oh, you know you can ask me a harder question than that!

Elation

(for my dear Hal)

For whatever it's worth I give thanks for sunlight between pines
especially tall, old red ones on the ridge between lakes

and purple Monrovia maples
down by the water

where we lay on our stomachs in the grass
and brushed our teeth in the cold spring

and sang loud songs from the old country
as much for the echo across the water

as for the beavers slapping their tails
just for our benefit

as we stood on the pier
conducting the wind and the waves and the cattails

as if we were Vivaldi
composing *The Four Seasons*

and all because we longed for that one day
we might actually get back there

to the land of childhood

and if we've been elated over the years
it always has something to do

with the way the wind sings through the meadow
or waxwings dart like sixteenth notes across the sky

and leaves flare against the horizon
like new love

just as the sun goes down
and night becomes sanctified in the presence of so many stars!

Addendum

And I ask myself, what is it, exactly about men with cherubic faces
And ruddy cheeks, curly hair that makes me absolutely swoon?
Who stand behind me in church and sing with the gusto of Gabriel
(and all the seraphim)
With such resonance that my bones vibrate with the thrill
And my eyes tear up every time?

My husband says they must remind me of him!
(and he may be right)
But certainly the young French horn player at the symphony was a
dead ringer
For a Greek dancer I once knew
And a child icon in a remote monastery
In the far reaches of Romania seemed to bear the same DNA

As the new grandson my daughter
Hands me at the baptism
Saying, "He is yours *and* mine"
So that the diapason of my heart
Swells with all possible Pythagorean semitones—
But I digress.

For this is not to rule out the Jewish doctor
Who breaks into song as he takes my pulse
Nor the African pharmacist
Who hums as he fills my prescriptions
Nor the tall, muscular Scotsman
Who can heft a thirty-pound stone
With incredible ease
As well as pipe the old mournful tunes

Nor the Dane who plays his mandolin with joy
Nor the proverbial Latin Lover (no comment)
Nor the British writer who can twist my heart strings
With his carefully crafted lines
Nor even the blind French composer
Whose accent suggests
He can see beyond the sighted to the soul—

So, no, they don't all remind me of him
Except for a certain look
That twinkles in his eye now and then
When he is up to certain mischief
And I can imagine the boy he once was

Perhaps like the one next door
Who professed his undying ardor
When I was still young enough to be embarrassed
By such effusiveness
But treasure still
Even though such proclamations
Grow fewer and farther between with the years

So, in the end, perhaps it's just a weakness I have
For guys with a sweet face
Who aren't afraid to be spontaneous and silly
Who can throw back their heads and sing
With such full-hearted fervor
No explanation could readily suffice.

Choosing Everything

The first snow on the lawn,
Sliver of moon in the sky—
Once, you said you loved me
All the way up there and back
And I mentioned the rings of Jupiter
And we both laughed
As our hearts danced
Like stars in their silver slippers
Dipping their toes
Into freezing water!!

Improvisation

(ode to Scott Joplin and all the unknown people of my birth family)

Lord knows
I want the heat of you
The wing, heartbeat, lub-dub
Blue hawk and soar
The backward dip
All trapeze swirl
And tricky jitter
Of bird-balance
Between two reeds
And the hard bass line
The hot steel
Rolling out of the foundry
A brain-vibrating blue
Major minor diminished augmented
White keys
Shouldering the black
And tight, tight coil of piano wire
Strung unstrung and restrung
Vibrato and the riff of you—
Heads back
And eyes closed
Charleston and Sunflower
Slow Drag
The downhome willows
Weeping
And maple leaf disjointed
Upside down
And drifting
In all
Directions.

Days Like This

What we spent all winter dreaming about—the sun high in the heavens and enough of a breeze to keep the zinnias coy in their ruffled collars well into October and you on the porch chair next to mine reminiscing about the time we swam all the way across the lake joking about swimming The English Channel when the wind and waves came up behind us and almost overtook us and God knows we would have let them because we were young then, our hearts always turbulent with anticipation and then you learned French and went off to Paris and I contemplated living in Russia but had to settle for reading Turgenev and the winters passed and for a great while we completely forgot about each other until now but even now a pointillist portrait of unasked questions and surrealist light still crowds the garden.

Whiskey, Neat.

(inspired by Archibold Motley's canvas *Blues*)

Somewhere Harlem and jazz-wailing
Saxophone-trumpet slow dance,
bass strum arrhythmia

And afterwards on the bed
Talking about all the places we'll go
Belize maybe, or Vegas

Neon flashing outside our hotel window
your hand flame on my hip
up my spine

as if there were anywhere else
we'd need to go . . . ever

then morning back beat to Penn Station.
overnight frost lifting its skirt
in all the shop windows

Jazz riff of linger,
concentric circles of light
On the floor of the terminal—

Terminal skylight sun announcing last train:

last kiss of lovers
leaning into concentric
last of the last. *Obligato.*

Your lips on mine   Linger-rush vibrato
Pulsing floor, walls, last train,

Funny how things
turn inside out! Flash!

Ironic how I was the one hated to leave.   Left

Only later realized your smile
          —skylight improv
Neon. Concentric

Hand-flame on my wrist, cheek
     Flatted fifth . . . last train
                                        mournful Clarinets

Love
(That Summer You Were Two)

That summer you were two
We sat on the bluff
Watching the comets
Fall from the sky
Onto the blanket of field and lake
And while the other children
Walked on water
Following the moon's path
To the far horizon
And back,
We filled our pockets to bursting
With stars upon stars
Enough for a thousand years of dreaming;
And while I told you little stories
About the faeries and constellations,
You fell asleep in my arms
So that I knew even then
That when you outgrew me—
Which of course you did all too soon—
I could still every so often
Always slip a star under your pillow
When you least expected
In hopes that when the day
We both secretly dreaded
Finally arrived
You might find a remaining few embers
Twinkling among my prized possessions—
Enough that you might always awake
Still smiling
Up at the sky.

Ode to Delirium

God knows I was hoping it'd be you
Who'd start the first soft kiss
But maybe it was me
Or maybe nothing ever happened
(All wishful thinking)
The green glass of your eyes
Melting in the sun
Me dizzy with the thought of love
(Whatever that is)
But it was summer
And the heat and clamor
Of cicadas, the city and its birds
And all the goings on
Of people in the streets
Should have been enough
But the way your hand
Held mine as we walked up
All those stairs to your apartment
Is what I most remember
The sound of your key
Turning in the lock
And the sudden wash of light
Through open windows
And all those places we met for love
And could never get enough of—
And the sparrows
Raucous in the trees
The thrush
With arias the likes of which
Must have made Vivaldi gasp,
The river's rush
With lust that defies description

Yet all the more seductive
For having been transcribed into a minor key,
All those sixteenth and thirty-second notes
And glassy arpeggios
Flying off the heart's lost pages
As if nothing in the world
Matters more than the velocity of swifts
Darting through the Esperanza trees,
Or love's hopeless flare
Again, again Always again.
In the evening sky
Fainting in the breeze.

First Love, Last

From the train,
Houses blur by
Graffiti on boxcars like Sanskrit
And a boy in red hat
Making tracks
In the snow—
I recall a time you "wrote" our names with your boots
On a snow-covered field
The blizzard obliterating everything
Especially your face
As the train sped by
And time disappeared in a cloud of whiteness.

Train Yard

(for Jeremy, Erich and Gus,
Ron and Eric Ryce)

It's the first of April and someone has lugged a very large box up from the basement and it's filled with toy trains from the Forties and enough track to get from Detroit to Chicago and hands are grabbing the box cars and cattle cars and cabooses (cabeese?) and from somewhere little paintbrushes materialize and we call a party and the people from upstairs come down and the folks in the apartment next door come over and before we know it the track is laid in one door and out the other and down the driveway and onto the sidewalk and we set to work on painting miniature graffiti and practicing our very best boxcar and engine noises while the neighbor children look on thinking we must be drunk or something especially when we make a conga line down to the corner and back pretending to be the box cars and engines and coal cars chanting *chugga chugga choo choo*. until the children finally join in and even an Uber driver pulls up and plays with us for a hot minute and someone pays him for the pizza and we all collapse in the grass reliving the best years of our childhood, telling our tall tales with our mouths crammed full of pepperoni and pepsi and the moon comes up over the two-family flats and the CNN rolls smoothly behind the elm trees its whistle in celebratory hoots as if we owned stock in Monopoly railroads or even laughter pharmaceuticals, laughter: the best medicine in the world!

Obstructed View

The day the elephants marched through Corktown and down Michigan Avenue, the crowds going wild inside Tiger Stadium with Gibby at bat and us in our obstructed view seats where we couldn't see diddly but what did that matter because we were crazy in love and had eyes only for each other even though our respective spouses and kids were there too, and God knows I've never been much for baseball—too much standing around—but that day I was giddy with the thought of extra innings and though you were initially a Padres fan, in the end, you were won over by the Champions and though we left before the crowds tore up half the turf for souvenirs, we followed the marching bands to the bar, pumping our fists when some rowdies turned over a cop car in the intersection, and later, much later, someone saw us kissing under a street lamp but what did that matter—at the time what mattered was the heat of the moment and though I've not seen you for years, and the stadium is gone, and no one who lives here can afford a ticket, every time I hear the roar of opening day, I fully expect to turn around and see you waiting to kiss my eyelids; and the hairs on the back of my neck stand up whenever I hear the crack of a bat on my grandson's team; so, I am reminded what a thrill it is to actually win from time to time and how love is in no way unlike a hot summer day at the circus, or the voice of Ernie Harwell, long dead now, over the radio and everyone cheering in the streets, revving their engines, windows down, bare feet on the dashboard as if we owned the world!

Obstructed View: Old Tiger Stadium, Detroit

painting by Dennis Cook

Love Song for My Lost City

Long-lost brothers and sisters
come sit with me on the steps of my city
listen as the music from the Irish's downstairs flat

mingles with the khoum in the Azar's upstairs flat
like star-crossed lovers,
come sit by me and share your reasons for staying

Is it the voices of the Supremes
resounding in the school hallways?
the counterpoint of Satchmo and Aretha wafting across the alley?

or is it how the elm trees
arch over the streets
making them as cool and shady as a gothic cathedral?

possibly you have overheard
the cicadas as they gossip in the branches?
witnessed the cardinals spread their tails like Chinese fans?

or perhaps you have watched as the children
touch each others' faces, delight in the hair
that feels different from their own?

Do you hear them chatter like birds as they play together?
little sparrows splashing in the sidewalk puddles!

Friends, come be with me for a while
linger over a supper of bread and soup
bring your bowl to my table

there is plenty for everyone
there will be laughter for dessert
good wine and dancing for your pleasure;

Do not dwell on the fact
that the wealthy are packing their bags
behind closed doors

have put For Sale signs in their windows
pay no attention to the bigots
who hide their fears behind false excuses and accusations

Good Friends, talk to me of the things you love
tell me your dreams for your children
and grandchildren

show me the pictures of your family, the photos you keep in your
    wallet
do not let the hot night keep you alone
in your apartment

come into my garden
sit down with me among the roses
breathe deeply of the peonies and forsythia

then come savor the raspberries with me
from the bushes planted by my grandmother
and my grandmother's grandmother

let us press the stains of our fingers together
our combined hope mingled, pulsing for the future of our city

and won't you sing me the songs from your childhood
tell me about the times when tears of laughter
wet your faces?

how the aunties
cradled you in their aprons
the uncles tickled you until you shrieked and begged for mercy?

My Friends, do not dwell on the things you cannot change
perhaps we can change them together

Let us not light the fires of envy and destruction
remember our promises to cherish each other

Good Neighbors, be calm when the Man raises his fist at you
when Whitey threatens to destroy you
it is your dignity they wish to steal from you

don't let them!
speak softly but speak in your own behalf;
be adamant on behalf of others.

Good neighbors, we must protect the women and children
pray for the teenagers and the leaders our nation,
for the talk show hosts to stop distorting, the politicians' lying

Let us turn off the noise of the televisions and cell phones
and instead plant new seeds in the garden
remind our children of our love for them as we discipline them
    fairly

Let us shelter the child
who has been abandoned;
speak out for the poor who cannot defend themselves

My sisters and brothers
may we remember the wounded
and bandage them when they are broken

let us not be afraid to put our hands on them
that they might be healed,
hold their hands when they are dying

Let us be kind to the strangers among us
welcome them to our table
enlist them to help rebuild our city

Dear Ones, let us resist the urge to speak out in anger
please be kind to yourself
when you are lonely

can we not gather to listen to the sounds of the wind in the
    branches?
to plant new trees by the water?
invite those who left to return to us and our city?

let us ask them to join us
on the steps of our city
to listen to its new music

Perhaps we can ask them to teach us
the words to their music
ask them to share their kind thoughts with us.

Let us remember to invite them to sit and chat with us on the steps
    of our city
ask them to forget their reasons for leaving
suggest they stay when the talk turns to silent

let us treasure the moments of thoughtful silence

Only then will we be able to ask them
to share with us their hopes and dreams for our city
only then will they be free to listen.

And then, Dear Ones, let your gaze linger before you leave my
    table
let me memorize your smiles and your laughter,
let me dream we might meet again with the sunrise.

Twice

Midsummer, summer's end
I see you coming toward me across the sand
Your hand a triangle of light
Raised in greeting!
And my heart, that feather
Lifts and dives
And strays
So far so fast
I cannot even think
To try to stop it!

Heart Song

(for everyone, named and unnamed, I have ever loved!)

I was following my heart
And there you were
Not knowing love could grow
But then I saw your eyes
Were filling with surprise
And now I know

The sting of Cupid's dart
The damage to the heart
The thrill it can impart
But then I saw surprise
Was smiling in your eyes
And now I know

I can't let go
The smile in your eyes
Could grow and grow
The love song in your heart
The longing it would start
This is the great surprise
And here we go

Birthday RSVP

Though statistics tell us we can expect a 20% return,
all 25 third grade Jedi have *rizzvipped*
and here they are at the door right on time,
one in tears and parents telling us we're crazy,
some with worried looks,

but the January weather is in our favor
and first off, the mummy game exceeds all expectations,
followed by a pirate relay and some spinning race I made up at the
last minute
and I'm thinking what was I thinking? a vintage party can be fun
and didn't we do this when we were kids, the yard soggy
and the sun like a birthday balloon in the bright sky?

and once back indoors for Bingo and Pin the Tail,
only five pieces of chocolate cake get ground into the carpet,
only three sodas spilled and thank god flavored waters don't stain
and except for the two little terrorists whose heads I'd like to
knock together,
who pull every toy out of the closet I forgot to lock,
darts whizzing past my head like Falcon Millenia
and the five-year-old who says he hates pizza,
and two who *NEVER* drink water—
things go remarkably well:

the decibel level never much louder than the Original Star Wars
Movie!

and while the guest of honor sits in the middle of the circle,
his gifts perfectly aligned like the planets are supposed to be this
very night,
the silly ones get everyone to blow their party blowers with their
nostrils

and three hours later all the parents arrive for the pick-up right on schedule
if you can believe that! (two exceptions, though I'm not saying who)

and when all is said and done we collapse
and watch the rerun of Han Solo and Chewbaca
getting the medals I think
I so richly deserve!

Late Afternoon

We give up waiting for the sky to clear
And go inside, each to our own tasks—
You to the sports channel
The kids to Sponge Bob
And me to a book by a favorite author
And for a while
The sound of rain on the roof
Puts us all to sleep
You dreaming of the Carpathians
In your natural language
And the kids of their next birthday
And me wandering through
My childhood of nameless
Places hoping somewhere
There might be a family
That is more than I yet know
And feeling the music of their names
As if they are already
Inside me

Arrival

(for Jeremy, Nik, and Maya)

The night you were born I'd been up late washing walls and joking about the nesting instinct and other old wives tales and when I finally collapsed into bed around 2am your father said whatever you do don't go to the hospital tonight I have that interview in the morning and no sooner did I reassure him than the water broke and we were on our way city streets blooming with yellow street lamps and rain dancing on the windshield and when we arrived, the doctor was already waiting with a team of medical students faces gleaming with anticipation at witnessing their first birth the doctor cheering at certain intervals and your father breathing in sync with me the way we'd practiced in Lamaze classes and then suddenly you at my breast already the size of a two-month old all eleven pounds of you and your sister asking if you could say your ABCs and me glad for an extra two days of sleep while you stayed under a bilirubin lamp and even to this day photos of your father in yellow hospital gown looking both stunned and weary as if trying to answer those interview questions in his head.

And now the day is here that I need to tell your own children about that glorious night but you are so far away and have been gone so long now that I would be wise to write it all down and send this and all those other wonderful and funny and terrible stories in birthday letters in hopes they won't get lost while I dream of holding them in my arms and kissing their little cheeks and the wisps of hairs at the back of their necks and wishing there had been a way I could have been there to dance them around the NICU in those days when you and your wife were so stunned with worry and exhaustion you couldn't sleep but I am grateful for Skype and these days for Zoom and Face Time and, yes, for Frequent Flyer miles and even for delays and for stopovers and especially for your willingness to meet me at the airport at all hours and for lifelong friends who understand the long, long trip with all of its heartbreak and joy.

Bleeding Hearts

Though I'd heard of them
I swear I'd never once even seen them

But the first time I stumbled across them
Recognized them for exactly what they were

Their little faces sweet and red
With embarrassment, shame and pride

And when I exclaimed over them, the boy I was with
Picked one and placed it behind my ear

Saying they would always
Remind him of me;

So of course I fell instantly in love
But then he disappeared to a girl back home

And though once several years later
He sent me an unexpected bouquet,

I never heard from him after that.

dicentra spectabilis got its name for its pillow-like, heart-shaped flower that dangles like a single pendulous drop. Bleeding hearts are shade-loving woodland plants that bloom in the cool of spring. Although they stay in bloom for several weeks, the plants often become ephemeral, disappearing for the rest of the summer if exposed to too much sun or heat. The roots stay alive and the plant will regrow in fall or the following spring

I Never Thought

I'd lose you
But yes
you've gone ahead now and
Exactly what I knew would
But so soon
and yet
You'll find
your heart
No afterthought
because elation
Even though my footprints
in this tide pool disappearing
You no longer tied
to me
Your hand pulling
sudden!
out of mine
And yet the moon,
its newest self here
Laughing in the tide
water
Stretching out its light,
its life ribbon
Between us.

Ode to Sandy Hook

When the wind makes a mockery of the things you fear most and the mundane light from the cell phone makes a blue triangle on the blanket covering your bed by the window, you sleep the sleep of exhaustion only to dream of making a rubbing of the name on your son's gravestone and you wake exhausted knowing you've slept an eternity in three hours only to wake knowing the truth you'd hoped to escape from is still the truth and all the children whose parents laid them next to your own boy will never get past seven will never know if they could have been university students or professors or president or parents of boys much like themselves and you reach out to them in their long sleep willing them to turn to you but you have turned to stone you are a monument to all that is unspoken because there are no words to return to, no words to speak the unspeakable.

High Tide

Largo: Just now at the window   wind slipping over the sill and into the bed
flare of clouds just after sunset and deep intoxicating kiss
under a certain tree just like the one a shy boy from down the street
once kissed me under

Low Tide

Tonight the moon sloshes around our ankles
Beads of light rippling like little fishes
And stars overhead winking,
Winking at their own jokes
And then the wind
Suddenly out of nowhere
Whistling an old zydeco tune
Between its teeth
Making the cedar on the bluff
Unfold its branches
Like an accordion
And the chill-warm breeze insisting
We have no choice
But to peel off our clothes
And plunge into the last deep blue
Surge of desire.

The Day Sky Is Also Filled with Stars

Those few short summers I could walk through a cathedral of trees,
up a dirt path and out to the south pasture for blueberries—
except for the one time I saw a bear—
but mostly, I longed for the breeze to pick up
so I could stand at the end of the dock
with Vivaldi on my headphones
and conduct the waves and the reed grass
while the wind lifted the water and clouds
so forcefully but wistfully I could be Zubin Mehta,
or Leonard Bernstein, or Tar! leading the Philharmonic,
so deep was I in each note
and in thoughts of a boy/girl back home
who was so flamboyant and vigorous that some laughed at him/her
but others understood they had a contemplative side;
and though I say I can't remember their name,
I nevertheless longed for them to notice me,
to walk with me through the maiden grass to the top of the dune
and sit looking out over the afternoon
and I would say to them things such as *see how you have ruined*
my heart,
how you have broken me
or perhaps they would tell me that the day sky is also filled with
stars
and maybe our fingers would touch or maybe not
as we listened for the thrush
and its glassy arpeggios
while evening draped its pale blue scarf over us
and the sun eased itself, laughing, slowly into the water.

I Think of You in That Faraway City

I've been to only once
Expecting sun and warmth
But it was cold, people
Wearing down jackets in July

And I know how vulnerable you are out there alone
Without me, the wind
Coming in off the ocean,
The bridge gleaming

With all the fool's gold of youth—
The confidence that everything is as it seems—
That you will still be safe

Even if you don't lock the door
To your apartment,
That the boy you live with
Will bring you no harm.

Perhaps I was never nineteen after all
Perhaps the wind did not lift
That bride's veil that I hated
But that my mother insisted on

Perhaps the worry
Written on her forehead
Was not a frown
But a tiara of unspoken pain

Of too much knowledge
That comes only with the years
And that we are so much better
Simply not thinking about

(Let alone mentioning)

And so I send you a cheerful text
Wishing you morning birdsong
And a cat to sleep upon your feet
And a dog to escort you

Safely to your class and back
And dreams to be fulfilled
When you least of all expect.

I Think You Were Eight That Summer

Tearing through the dunes on your dirt bike and learning to fish off the pier,
The afternoon you convinced me you could be safe without me hovering,

You took your pole and tackle box
Down to the water where you

Put on a lifejacket and hunkered
Down in the reeds

Waiting for a fish, any fish
To swim in your direction

And as the sun rose in the sky
And sweat gathered on your nose

I was certain you would give up
But after a few hours

Decided maybe I should go look for you
Just to make sure you were safe

But just as I got to the top of the hill
Saw you running in my direction

Breathless, shouting, “Mom! Mom!
I caught a hundred fish!”

And though I’d heard the fish
Were biting like nobody’s business

That July, when I asked you
Where they were, those hundred fish,

Thinking you'd lead me to the water's edge,
you set down your tackle box near the cattails

And opened the lid and with great pride
Exclaimed, "They're here!!

And then I saw you'd taken the lures
Out of their plastic cases

And inserted the tiny bluegills and minnows
That were just the right size.

And though we laughed with delight.
Your glee was based on something

Quite different from mine
And though I doubt we fixed them

For dinner we had such fun
Telling everyone what an incredible catch

You'd made as you held up each
Little box, proof! for everyone to see

The laughter and applause
Worth every minute

Of an afternoon in
The hot and baking sun!

Child of My Heart

Gone now of his own volition
His cheerful boy's voice suddenly a man's—
The piano silent, the piper's bag
Locked in its case,
The daily walk together
Ended now for now
The sword and fencing glove
Outgrown and set aside
The iBook and iPhone and coding words
And programmes now
The lingua franca of his deepest desires;
And though he has tried to teach me
The nuances, I have failed ever so miserably.

Wind, in Three Parts

Part 1: The Wind Is Rushing East

Scattering a confetti of stars
Across the water
The children in the street
Kicking stones toward the school
River of children rushing, some loitering,
Some of them turn back to look at me
But when I try to catch up
They dart off like fireflies—
I knew all of their names once, first and last
(Some of them might still remember mine)
They were singing a patriotic song
The word, *flag,* a high note
I knew all of the songs once, the words,
Because the music teacher complimented me,
I tried hard to impress her
I knew all of the words then,
Sometimes I still do.

Part 2: The Wind Is in the Tall Grass

Once, a boy and I sat in the tall grass
Singing the word, *love,* to each other
Pretending to be opera stars

But then he ran off without me—
And I have searched everywhere
Calling his name into the wind

But the wind is a river
Some days it sings the songs
From the Old Country,

Songs the grandparents sang in the fields
Sang to us when we were children
How they waved to us so happy to see us

After what seemed to them a long time
And all these years we rushed off
Without them, couldn't understand the old ways

Didn't want to
The wind always rushing
Here and there

Sometimes sideways,
Calling our names, echoing through the tall grass
The grandparents always waving.

Somewhere there is a boy—
May he some day
Turn and remember

the wind in the tall grass
How I called after him
How it still shouts and whispers his name.

Part 3: The Wind Is Always Rushing

The Wind is always rushing
Carrying us away
When we lie down in the tall grass

It steals the memories
From our hearts' pockets
Tosses them to the sky like confetti

But when we try to catch them
Steals them away again—
Once there was a boy who said he loved me

But then he ran on ahead
And I could never find him after that.
Neither of us was ever the same again.

Finale: Some Mornings

Some mornings the river
Is glass
The sunlight tricking us
Into thinking we can
See through a magic mirror
See the carp beneath the water
See the flash of fin and tail
The big one
That always eludes us in the end
Just like the words we've been
Meaning to say but really can't
Not that they’re not there waiting
Just that they get too slippery
Get away before they get caught.

The Road to Anywhere

(for Pete and all good friends who died too soon)

Now that we've come here
The leaves are telling us
This is the right place
The branches point in all directions
So even if we get lost
We won't be lost forever
The road to the sky is a good one
But so is the limb
That stretches out over the sea
And the moonbeams
That lead straight to your heart
And back
Even if just for thirty-seven seconds at a time;

So now I think I finally understand
How you can leave without regret
Without even thinking to say goodbye
Because we can still
Sometimes find each other
When least expected
In the flicker of light,
In the tiniest of leaves
Curled tightly against the wind
Opening to blue
Exquisite sky.

Love Me Again

Let the wind sing the sound of your name in the trees
Let the warm breeze
Drift through my window at night
The curtains gasp with delight
And let the spring rain
Whisper its millions of promises
From you to me and back again
May the flowers nod in approval
And the clouds laugh
Like they used to
Because my reflection in your eyes
Was deep and clear and unfettered
And the river ran loud
And wild
And free.

Eleven, Twelve, Dig and Delve

and even after they have outgrown me I understand
as far as silence goes   somewhere birds
might still be singing

About the Author

Alinda Dickinson Wasner's work has appeared in 70+ small press print and online literary anthologies, including *Amelia Press Review, Ararat, Atlanta Review, Avatar, Black Mountain, Black Mountain Press' Sixty-Four Best Poets of 2021, Comstock Review, Camroc Press Review, Connecticut River Review, Cortland Review, Crab Orchard, December Mag, Evening Street, Gemini Magazine, Halcyon, Making Waves: West Michigan Review, Michigan Natural Resources, Michigan Jewish History Jl, Mountain Troubador, Naugatuck River Review, New Milennium Writers, The Orchards Poetry Journal, Outsider Writers, Passages North, Poetry Pacific, Spillway, Third Wednesday, Wayne Review, Wittenberg Review, Southward Literary Jl of Ireland, Raven's Perch, Sports Literate, SUNY Literary Jl, Up the Staircase, Khorus Jl of Greek Dance and Arts,* among others.

She is the winner of many literary prizes, including several Tompkins Awards, Wittenberg University Writer's Award, Atlanta Review Prize, Mr. Cogito Press Award, Chicago Poetry Center juried prize, MacGuffin prize, Metro Times award, Judith Siegal Pearson prize, Paumonauk Poetry prize, Red Planet, Vermont Poetry Society prize, and a Prague Writer's fellowship, among others. In 2015, she received 2nd place in Ireland's International Poetry Prize out of 2,000 entrants.

She was also nominated for the 2011 Best of the Net Award and won the 2019 and 2020 Springfied Arts Poetry Prize.

Her collection, *Still Burning* (2015), is available from Ex Libris, Amazon, and B&N. A chapbook, *When You don't Know Who You Are,* is available from Crisis Chronicle's Press, Cleveland and Amazon. Another chapbook, *Kissing the Ikons,* is available from Finishing Line Press. A new collection, *Heart Houdini,* is forthcoming from May Apple Press in 2024. A chapbook, *Departures, Arrivals,* by Ridgeway Press is out of print.

Listed in *Poets and Writers,* Wasner lives and writes in metro Detroit.

Other poems can be found on her blog:
thestarvingpoet.com

Praise for *The Day Sky Is Also Filled with Stars*

Alinda Wasner's brilliantly crafted collection is a generous, intimate journey of the heart that makes the labor of love seem so organic even the most hardened heart will be seduced. Of her children she writes: . . . *I fell so deeply, madly/in love I shall/ never be able to extract myself /from myself.* Wasner explores love at first sight, love of family, her house, her city, but not without regarding the risks of grief and loss. *Like the moon on late night water/ My memory of you keeps breaking:/ First light, then shadow/And always/ The unbearable space/ That holds the two/ Together.* You hear the music, exquisite details of nature imbued with arias of love, and feel/: *somewhere the wind/ waiting/ With its kiss.* Wasner's poems convey earned wisdom, not only of the heart, but our shared humanity. *The Day Sky Is Also Filled with Stars* is a perfect collection for our challenging times-one you'll return to to be reminded of abundance that surrounds us. As Wasner puts it: *The way to be happy is to always be in love*, and she backs it up, beautifully.

Diane DeCillis, *When the Heart Needs a Stunt Double* (Wayne State University Press)

The Day Sky Is Also Filled with Stars, Alinda Wasner's capacious, buoyant, collection, is a tribute to those who matter most in life, giving poetic expression to the relationships that we all (if we are lucky) cherish most. Readers will soar through this lavish memoir-in-poems reveling in the copious gifts of family and friends, joy and grief that can make the heart resound "as if dreams tunneled under." A triumphant collection filled with wit and heart and pure delight, I LOVED this beautiful work. Pure bliss.

Kelly Fordon, Michigan podcast hostesss, Springfed Arts instructor, Midwest Book Award Finalist and Eric Hoffer Book Award Finalist, *I Have the Answer* and *Garden for the Blind* (Wayne State University Press)

"Love is a Carnival," Alinda Wasner offers as root note to *The Day Sky Is Also Filled with Stars.* Life's carnal pleasures, love and marriage, and grief, are grounded by the chainlink movement of parent to child to parent and poem to poem. Wasner writes with intoxication and joy, noticing the small things that give our human and natural world resonance. Brush the rice from the bed, Dear Reader, because *The Day Sky* offers an abundance of lyrical kisses.

Dennis Hinrichsen, Professor Emeritus, Greater Lansing Poet Laureate, *Rip-Tooth, Kurosawas' Dog,* and *Fleshplastique and Schemageometrica*

In *The Day Sky Is Also Filled with Stars,* Alinda Wasner explores tender, intergenerational love in spare and precise detail. Mischief, wonder, the hum of an afternoon radio left on a sill—every page suggests stolen moments and lost places, cut from the chaos and quiet of family life. Friends and lovers come and go, demolished schools reappear, and the poetry of a grandchild's questions, faithfully preserved, is lifted into place alongside them. Delightful.

James Macmillen, Detroit poet, winner, InsideOut Literary Arts 2022 Poetry Prize

Detroit poet Alinda Wasner writes with clear-eyed resolve about love in all its myriad permutations, as her poems lead us, in the end, through the forest and brambles of love and loss, life and longing, holding our hearts and hands the entire way.

Caroline Maun, Editor, *Third Wednesday,* Wayne State University professor and English Department chair

www.ingramcontent.com/pod-product-compliance
Lightning Source LLC
LaVergne TN
LVHW020628100826
845148LV00012B/2099

* 9 7 8 1 6 3 9 8 0 3 8 4 2 *